D0977106

Dear

-------------------------------------,

I've promised that

*I Will Love You Forever.*

I'm keeping that promise.

I love you!

-------------------------------------

# I Will

# Love You

THOMAS NELSON
*Since 1798*

NASHVILLE   DALLAS   MEXICO CITY   RIO DE JANEIRO   BEIJING

© 2007 by Thomas Nelson

Published in Nashville, TN, by Thomas Nelson. Thomas Nelson is a trademark of Thomas Nelson, Inc.

Thomas Nelson, Inc., titles may be purchased in bulk for educational, business, fundraising, or sales promotional use. For information, please email SpecialMarkets@ThomasNelson.com.

All scripture references are from the New King James Version of the Bible (NKJV) ©1979, 1980, 1982, 1992, Thomas Nelson, Inc., Publisher. Used by permission. All rights reserved.

Designed by Lookout Design, Stillwater, Minnesota

ISBN-10: 1-4041-0504-2
ISBN-13: 978-14041-0504-1

Printed in China

# Table of Contents

# Introduction

*I will love you forever.* Only one person fully understands this remarkable vow and knows how to keep it. He can promise forever love because He is forever love (Psalm 136; Jeremiah 31:3). He's the Lord of all eternity (Psalm 145:3-4, 13), and He never changes (James 1:17).

If you want to know how love is really supposed to be, you have to go to its Source. The wisdom in this book comes from God. When you and your spouse apply this advice to your marriage, your relationship will become stronger and more beautiful than you ever dreamed possible. As you walk through the myriad circumstances and changes in life, you will have the assurance of God's guidance. You will know what it is to love and be loved forever.

# 1 JOHN 4:7-12, 16

*Beloved, let us love one another, for love is of God; and everyone who loves is born of God and knows God. He who does not love does not know God, for God is love. In this the love of God was manifested toward us, that God has sent His only begotten Son into the world, that we might live through Him. In this is love, not that we loved God, but that He loved us and sent His Son to be the propitiation for our sins. Beloved, if God so loved us, we also ought to love one another. No one has seen God at any time. If we love one another, God abides in us, and His love has been perfected in us. . . . And we have known and believed the love that God has for us. God is love, and he who abides in love abides in God, and God in him.*

# Learning to
# Love

## Gold

All the gold and silver in the world is not worth
as much as the abiding true love of a husband or
wife. Give your love as a precious gift to the
one worthy of your care and affection.

### PSALM 68:13

*You will be like the wings of a dove
covered with silver,
And her feathers with yellow gold.*

# Trust

Let your beloved know that your loyalty and fidelity can be trusted. Trust is one key to a happy bonding of your love. Cultivate trust and you cultivate a fulfilling and refreshing love life.

## PROVERBS 31:11

*The heart of her husband safely trusts her,*
*So he will have no lack of gain.*

9

# Virtue

Virtue is the foundation of a solid marriage.
Let your beloved know that his or her love
and affection are safely entrusted to you.
Don't give in to the temptation to squander
your love irresponsibly.

### PROVERBS 31:10

*Who can find a virtuous wife?*
*For her worth is far above rubies.*

# Garden

Love is like a garden. The seed of love is
planted, but unless someone tends the
garden a strong plant will never grow.
Love requires long, hard work.
Pay attention every day to your beloved.

### SONG OF SOLOMON 4:16

*Let my beloved come to his garden
And eat its pleasant fruits.*

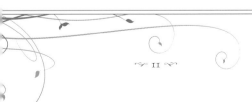

# Words

Words can build a relationship or destroy it. Let your words be those that build honesty and love between you and your beloved. Speak from your heart and your love will be healthier for it.

## PROVERBS 16:24

*Pleasant words are like a honeycomb,*
*Sweetness to the soul and health to the bones.*

# Nighttime

May your nights be filled with the
comfort of a binding love. Don't let the
troubles of your day intrude upon the
coziness of a night spent in the arms
of your beloved.

## PROVERBS 7:18

*Come, let us take our fill of love until morning;*
*Let us delight ourselves with love.*

# Kindness

Kindness builds love. Act in a kindly
manner that seeks the good of the one you
love. Show your love by thinking of your
mate first before yourself. You'll find a
reward beyond your imagination if your
love follows this noble path.

## ROMANS 12:9-10

*Let love be without hypocrisy.*
*Abhor what is evil. Cling to what is good.*
*Be kindly affectionate to one another.*

# Forever

True love weathers every storm and
outlasts every trouble. Make your love the
kind of love that shelters you forever.
Build a relationship with your beloved that
will comfort you in your old age.

## PROVERBS 5:19

*As a loving deer and a graceful doe,*
*Let her breasts satisfy you at all times;*
*And always be enraptured with her love.*

# One Mind

Seek harmony in your relationship with your loved one. Don't take detours to total agreement. Talk about your differences until there is full understanding. Do not be afraid of a healthy compromise. Live with your beloved in peace.

## 2 Corinthians 13:11

*Be of good comfort, be of one mind, live in peace; and the God of love and peace will be with you.*

# Bonded

God is the One who joined you together
with your beloved. He is the One who
ordained marriage between a man and a
woman. If you need guidance in your
marriage, and you will, ask it from the One
who abundantly and freely gives.

## MATTHEW 19:6

*Therefore what God has joined together,*
*let not man separate.*

# Growing
# Together

## Goodness

God crowns each year of our life with His goodness. His mercy and love cushion us from life's blows. His care goes before us, and He prepares a way for us through all our days.

### PSALM 65:11

*You crown the year with Your goodness,*
*And Your paths drip with abundance.*

# Fruitfulness

As a new day begins, remember God
has brought you and your loved one
together for a life of joy and
fruitfulness. Don't settle for less.

PSALM 92:14

*They shall still bear fruit in old age;*
*They shall be fresh and flourishing.*

# *Families*

Thank God for your friends and family.
The bonds of love that drove you to each
other are blessed by God. He wants you to
rejoice in the ties of love He has given you.

### PSALM 68:6

*God sets the solitary in families;*
*He brings out those*
*who are bound into prosperity,*
*But the rebellious dwell in a dry land.*

# Prayer

Prayer cements your heart to the heart of your beloved. Take time to pray with the special one you love. In praying, you draw near to the soul of the one who means so much to you.

## MATTHEW 18:20

*For where two or three are gathered together in My name,
I am there in the midst of them.*

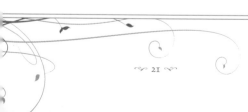

# Choices

Love has its price. When you stand
with your beloved you cannot always
stand with the rest of the world. But it
is the willingness to make the choice
that is a sign of true love.

## GENESIS 2:24

*Therefore a man shall leave*
*his father and mother*
*and be joined to his wife,*
*and they shall become one flesh.*

# Seed

Your love grows from a seed God planted in your heart. No one succeeds in truly loving another unless God gives you that ability. It is God who makes your love flourish. Remember Him in worship and prayer.

PSALM 92:13

*Those who are planted in the house of the LORD*
*Shall flourish in the courts of our God.*

# Warmth

Lying in bed with your loved one keeps you
warm through all of life's seasons.
When you are together in your intimacy,
you can forget the storms that rage outside.
So draw near to each other and be warm.

ECCLESIASTES 4:11

*Again, if two lie down together,*
*they will keep warm;*
*But how can one be warm alone?*

# Sharing

Share your troubles with your beloved.
Together you can work to turn your troubles
into triumphs. No one is able to do alone
what two can do together, especially when it
comes to prayer.

## GENESIS 25:21

*Now Isaac pleaded with the LORD for his wife,*
*because she was barren;*
*and the LORD granted his plea.*
*And Rebekah his wife conceived.*

# Scripture

Don't neglect the reading of God's Word
with your beloved. Spending time together
getting to know God better is one of the
richest joys you will know as a couple.
His Word will delight and strengthen you.

## PSALM 119:140

*Your word is very pure;*
*Therefore Your servant loves it.*

# Joined

God made wedding vows as strong as
steel and fragile as cut glass.
Protect and honor the promises you've
made to your beloved. Don't let anyone
come between you and your spouse.

## MARK 10:9

*Therefore what God has joined together,*
*let not man separate.*

# Comforting
# Each Other

## *Together*

You don't need to bear your troubles all alone.
Speak openly to your beloved about the deepest
concerns of your heart. Then together go to God
in prayer asking Him to lift your burden and ease
your anxiety. Let a gracious and loving Savior
help you with your every challenge.

### PSALM 55:22

*Cast your burden on the LORD,*
*And He shall sustain you.*

# Encouragement

Don't comfort your beloved from a standpoint of weakness. Be strong. Have courage. Speak the truth in love. Comfort your spouse in a way that brings encouragement. Help build on strengths that already exist. Remember, life has many seasons, and troubles come and go. You always have reason to hope.

## 1 THESSALONIANS 5:11

*Therefore comfort each other and edify one another, just as you also are doing.*

# Impossible

Don't give up hope when the dreams you have for you and your beloved seem impossible. God enjoys helping you make your dreams come true. Talk to Him about what is on your heart. Do it now.

### MARK 10:27

*With men it is impossible, but not with God;*
*for with God all things are possible.*

# Submission

When you find it difficult to be patient because
of conflicts you are experiencing with your mate,
remember God has asked you to maintain your
love relationship in spite of these challenges.
Be patient and help ease the troubles of the one
you love. Read 1 Corinthians 13 to help put
your relationship back on course.

## EPHESIANS 5:22, 25

*Wives, submit to your own husbands, as to the Lord....*
*Husbands, love your wives, just as Christ also loved the*
*church and gave Himself for her.*

# Healing

You never need to fix the pieces of a broken heart alone. Take your sadness to friends, and especially to that best Friend who sticks closer than a brother, Jesus Christ. He promises to heal the wounds of those who call Him Lord.

PSALM 34:18

*The LORD is near to those who have*
*a broken heart.*

# Gladness

Every marriage has its ups and downs.
No man or woman has ever been
perfect in their love. As you recognize
your own humanity, ask God to take
the hurts in your relationship and show
you and your beloved how to turn your
greatest challenges into triumphs.

### PSALM 30:11

*You have turned for me*
*my mourning into dancing;*
*You have put off my sackcloth*
*and clothed me with gladness.*

# Rest

God never suggested He would take away all
your burdens in life. You and your beloved will
both struggle until the days you die.
This is simply the formula known as life! But
God has promised to make your burdens lighter
never to give you more than you can bear, and to
give you His divine rest as you carry them.

## MATTHEW 11:28

*Come to Me, all you who labor and are heavy laden,
and I will give you rest.*

# Needs

Don't engage in excessive worry about your daily needs. God watches over all His creation, and He sees and knows what is vital for your sustenance. Come to Him with your beloved and tell Him of the things you need each day. Come to Him in faith—believing He will do what He promises.

## MATTHEW 6:30

*Now if God so clothes the grass of the field, which today is, and tomorrow is thrown into the oven, will He not much more clothe you, O you of little faith?*

# Safely

God promises you and your beloved a safe dwelling place in Him. Bring your hurts and disappointments to your loving Father who wants only His best for you. Don't try to face life all on your own. Live your life by living and loving together.

## PROVERBS 1:33

*But whoever listens to me will dwell safely,*
*And will be secure, without fear of evil.*

# Agreement

Loneliness can weigh heavily on you when you face a difficult decision. If you and your mate cannot agree on the path you are about to take, agree to disagree without pulling away from each other.

## MATTHEW 18:19

*Again I say to you that if two of you agree on earth concerning anything that they ask, it will be done for them by My Father in heaven.*

# Accepting
# One Another

## Captivate

Love captivates the beloved and holds it with soft
bonds of affection. Thoughts of personal desires
and freedoms pale beside the promise of
plunging to the depths of another heart and
spirit. This is what true, selfless love is all about.

### SONG OF SOLOMON 6:3

*I am my beloved's,*
*And my beloved is mine.*

# *Wrongs*

True love doesn't keep score of the wrongs
of another. If you continue to tally the
wrongs of your beloved and refuse to let
go of the past, you simply cannot grow
into a relationship filled with grace and
forgiveness. Forgive and forget. You will
both be winners in the long run.

## PSALM 130:3-4

*If You, LORD, should mark iniquities,*
*O Lord, who could stand?*
*But there is forgiveness with You.*

# Change

True love must stretch like rubber when
personal growth begins to take place.
Give your beloved room to be God's whole,
complete person. Be an encourager and not a
discourager. Recognize that change is an
important part of development.

## 1 CORINTHIANS 13:4

*Love suffers long and is kind;*
*love does not envy;*
*love does not parade itself, is not puffed up.*

# *Irritation*

Love is the balm that helps ease the friction of life between two people who have made a lifelong commitment to each other's growth and development. You and your spouse are unique individuals, not the same person. That's what drew you together in the first place. Don't let irritation over differences spoil the pleasure you have with your beloved. Apply the healing balm of love often. Start right now.

### PROVERBS 19:13

*The contentions of a wife are a continual dripping.*

# Approval

Truth is a precious gift given freely to
you and your beloved. It's simply yours
for the taking. Telling the truth is the
key to being known by each other and
feeling the wondrous release of being
wholly approved of by your beloved.
With true approval lies great peace.

### 1 Corinthians 13:6

*[Love] does not rejoice in iniquity,
but rejoices in the truth.*

# Thoughts

Fill your mind with wondrous thoughts of
the good things God has given you and
your beloved—the life you share, the love
that draws you to each other, and the
faith that helps you grow.

## PHILIPPIANS 4:8

*Finally, brethren, whatever things are true,*
*whatever things are noble, whatever things are just,*
*whatever things are pure, whatever things are lovely,*
*whatever things are of good report,*
*if there is any virtue*
*and if there is anything praiseworthy—*
*meditate on these things.*

# Understanding

Love can easily be clouded over with discouragement and despair. Sometimes you will find yourself confused, not knowing which direction to turn for help in your relationship. The good news is that God promised to give you His understanding in all matters. Lean on Him for mercy and guidance.

### JAMES 1:5

*If any of you lacks wisdom, let him ask of God, who gives to all liberally and without reproach, and it will be given to him.*

# Heart

God has a cozy place for you and your
spouse in His fatherly heart. When you are
sad, He invites you to come to Him and
share your every burden. He will share His
heart with you and give you peace. Come
into His heart today and feel His love.

## 1 JOHN 4:16

*We have known and believed
the love that God has for us.
God is love,
and he who abides in love
abides in God,
and God in him.*

45

# Contagious

Love is wonderfully contagious.
God's loving-kindness to you can prompt
you to acts of loving-kindness to your
spouse. Let your whole household be
infected with the joy of loving.
Spread that joy today wherever you are
and in whatever you do.

## 1 JOHN 4:11

*Beloved, if God so loved us,*
*we also ought to love one another.*

# Perfection

God has provided marriage as one way for
His children to grow to perfection.
When someone knows you as well as your
spouse does, you can always run, but you can
never hide! Use your learning about one
another to encourage growth.

## 2 PETER 3:14

*Therefore, beloved, looking forward to these
things, be diligent to be found by Him in peace,
without spot and blameless.*

# Being Companions

## Concentrate

Love has many dimensions and can make
you more scattered or more centered.
Concentrate and seek to be of one mind
with your mate. Discuss what you both
want from your relationship and then pull
together to reach that goal.

### 1 PETER 3:8

*Finally, all of you be of one mind,*
*having compassion for one another;*
*love as brothers, be tenderhearted, be courteous.*

# Movement

Your love relationship orbits around God
even as the moon moves around the earth.
God keeps your relationship moving,
fluid, dynamic. Always remember that
your heavenly Father is the One behind all
the love you give and receive.

## PSALM 66:10

*For You, O God, have tested us;*
*You have refined us as silver is refined.*

# Rejoice

Savor the companionship you share with
your beloved. Breathe deeply of the
beautiful fragrance of your love. Rejoice in
the blessings you enjoy as a couple.

## PROVERBS 5:18

*Let your fountain be blessed,*
*And rejoice with the wife of your youth.*

# *Increase*

The first taste of love can strike you like
a thunderbolt. But the steady
companionship and friendship are what
make the first exhaustive moment of
passion grow into a love to endure for a
lifetime. Grow with your beloved.

1 THESSALONIANS 3:12

*And may the Lord make you increase
and abound in love to one another.*

# Salvation

Deep in the soul of every man and
woman is the desire to know God and
experience His divine love. Honor that
desire in your mate and make God the
cornerstone of your marriage.

## PSALM 70:4

*Let all those who seek You*
*rejoice and be glad in You;*
*And let those who love Your salvation*
*say continually,*
*"Let God be magnified!"*

# Romance

Live in the heart of your beloved.

Risk romance with the one you love.

Speak the poetry of your love even if the

words don't seem like polished gems to you.

Your lover will treasure the words.

## Song of Solomon 2:14

*O my dove, in the clefts of the rock,*

*In the secret places of the cliff,*

*Let me see your face,*

*Let me hear your voice;*

*For your voice is sweet,*

*And your face is lovely.*

# Separation

God sees the hidden heart of everyone.

Give your innermost thoughts to God in

prayer. Let Him help you and your mate

separate the good from the bad that you

might be more fruitful for Him.

## PSALM 14:2

*The LORD looks down from*

*heaven upon the children of men,*

*To see if there are any who understand,*

*who seek God.*

# Friendship

Love has many faces. Its most beautiful
countenance is the face of friendship.
Cultivate a deep, lasting friendship with
your beloved. Play together with abandon,
share your interests, take long walks, and
learn to be one heart in two bodies.

PROVERBS 17:17

*A friend loves at all times.*

# Righteous

When you love, your soul meets and
knows the good inside the soul of your
beloved. Nurture that which is righteous,
correct, and noble in your beloved . . .
and let your beloved encourage those
same qualities within you.

## PSALM 85:10

*Mercy and truth have met together;*
*Righteousness and peace have kissed.*

# Servanthood

True love doesn't worry about who is the boss. It doesn't keep score in the "whose turn is it now" game. True love rejoices in doing what is good for your beloved and in serving one another.

## MATTHEW 23:11

*But he who is greatest among you shall be your servant.*

# Working Together

## Commitment

The burdens of life may seem impossible. Every day you observe your own weaknesses and those of your beloved. Then you remember what brought you together in the first place. You recall that a couple in love can pull a heavier load together than each can pull alone. It's what commitment is all about.

PSALM 67:6

*Then the earth shall yield her increase;*
*God, our own God, shall bless us.*

# Support

True love is not easily embarrassed. Seek to help work out the plan God has for your beloved's life. Never allow the teasing or ridicule of others to stop you from being 100 percent supportive of your mate. Because when all is said and done, all you really have on earth is each other.

## GENESIS 6:8, 7:1

*Noah found grace in the eyes of the LORD. . . . Then the LORD said to Noah, "Come into the ark, you and all your household, because I have seen that you are righteous before Me in this generation."*

# Aging

An enduring, loving marriage is a
wondrous monument to the goodness of a
gracious Lord. As gray hairs appear and
your bodies start to slow down, let your
love for each other increase. Your life
together is your greatest work for God.

## PSALM 71:18

*Now also when I am old and grayheaded,*
*O God, do not forsake me,*
*Until I declare Your strength to this generation,*
*Your power to everyone who is to come.*

# Freedom

Thank God daily for the bountiful privileges
He has given to you and your spouse.
Consider what your marriage and family
would be like if you did not have the freedoms
you are able to enjoy together. Rejoice in
God's blessings. Be thankful for the liberties
you have in Christ and in your country.

### GALATIANS 5:1

*Stand fast therefore in the liberty
by which Christ has made us free.*

# Weakness

Not all work is done through strength.
Some of the best, most enduring work is
accomplished when two lovers are at the point
of their greatest weakness, both spiritually
and physically. Don't wait to be strong to do
what God wants you to do. Simply put your
hand to the task to be done today.

## PSALM 84:5

*Blessed is the man whose strength is in You,*
*Whose heart is set on pilgrimage.*

# *Best*

The best part of love is not its intelligence.
Love is notoriously blind. Nor does the best
part lie in its unending hope. No, the best part
of love is simply in its seeking the very best for
your mate—and wanting that best for your
beloved more than you desire it for yourself.

## 1 CORINTHIANS 13:2

*Though I have the gift of prophecy,*
*and understand all mysteries and all knowledge,*
*and though I have all faith,*
*so that I could remove mountains,*
*but have not love, I am nothing.*

# Generations

The desire to mate and build a family is
given to people from a God who said,
"Be fruitful and multiply; fill the earth"
(Genesis 1:28). It's vital you and your spouse
regard your child-rearing years as among the
most fulfilling work of your entire lives.
You are designing our world's future.

### PSALM 89:4

*Your seed I will establish forever,*
*And build up your throne to all generations.*

# Protection

Lie down in repose in the warmth of God's love. His power protects you so you can frolic with your beloved. He smiles when He sees the love that flows between you and your mate in your most tender moments.

## PSALM 84:11

*For the LORD God is a sun and shield;*
*The LORD will give grace and glory;*
*No good thing will He withhold*
*From those who walk uprightly.*

# Individuals

God has made you and your mate as
individuals. He gave each of you different
talents and abilities. Ask Him how He would
like you to use these gifts in His service.
Always use your gifts to glorify the Lord!

PSALM 119:73

*Your hands have made me and fashioned me;*
*Give me understanding, that I may learn*
*Your commandments.*

# Tapestry

Love is a golden thread that, when woven
throughout your days, makes your life a
beautiful tapestry for all to see. Don't ration
the love you share with your mate.
Give your love freely—with an almost
reckless abandon. Let your love be a pleasant
blend of all that is wonderful and good.

## PSALM 37:4

*Delight yourself also in the LORD,*
*And He shall give you the desires of your heart.*

# Being Known

## *Known*

Your soul cries out to be known by someone special. And even as you are drawn to a deeper, more intimate relationship with your mate, a loving God chooses to draw you both closer to Himself. Your heavenly Father wants to be known, loved, and served. Live in the comfort of knowing your Father cares.

### PSALM 69:13

*But as for me, my prayer is to You,*
*O LORD, in the acceptable time;*
*O God, in the multitude of Your mercy,*
*Hear me in the truth of Your salvation.*

# Imperfection

Sing softly of your beloved's virtues.
Praise all good things. Let your pride be
seen on your face. Let your love for your
spouse be a hiding place for your
beloved's imperfections.

## COLOSSIANS 3:14

*But above all these things put on love,*
*which is the bond of perfection.*

# Searching

Gaze upon the sleeping face of your beloved.
When you were courting, words were not
enough to describe your mate's inner and outer
beauty. And after all this time, you still want to
know your beloved in greater depth. Keep the
exploration alive today and every day. Never be
satisfied. Always know there is more to be
discovered about your beloved.

## PROVERBS 20:27

*The spirit of a man is the lamp of the LORD,*
*Searching all the inner depths of his heart.*

# Speech

To some, love comes in a whisper. For others, it
arrives with great tumultuous shouts!
But from the beginning words were important.
Words either build or destroy. Let your
positive, loving speech—coupled with "love
actions"—be the proof of your love.

### COLOSSIANS 4:6

*Let your speech always be with grace, seasoned with salt,*
*that you may know how you ought to answer each one.*

# Criticism

Loving criticism is better than lying praise.
The one purifies so wounds can heal.
The other maintains a false peace while
wounds are allowed to worsen. Speak the
truth with your mate. Do not shy away
from caring, honest reproofs.

## PROVERBS 27:6

*Faithful are the wounds of a friend,*
*But the kisses of an enemy are deceitful.*

# *Appreciate*

Wedding days are rapturous and exciting.
Congratulations and happy tears abound. But
the wedding day ecstasy cannot endure
forever. Each twenty-four hours has its own
value. Like a game of chess, no challenge or
day is ever the same. Enjoy the difference.
Appreciate the variety of your love.

## ECCLESIASTES 7:10-12

*Do not say, "Why were the former days better than these?"*
*For you do not inquire wisely concerning this.*
*Wisdom is good with an inheritance . . .*
*But the excellence of knowledge*
*is that wisdom gives life to these who have it.*

# Politeness

True politeness is grounded in considerate
truth. When seeking to know your beloved,
don't be content with anything less than
straightforward, honest communication.
The roots of true love grow deeply when the
truth is spoken with compassion and love.

## Psalm 34:13

*Keep your tongue from evil,*
*And your lips from speaking deceit.*

# Treasure

Look at the face of your beloved and
you will see flashes of gold. But in fact
what you see is much more precious
than gold. A love rooted and grounded
in God makes your love's countenance
shine more than any earthly treasure.

## LUKE 12:34

*For where your treasure is,*
*there your heart will be also.*

# Light

A love that refuses to show its face is worthless. Without action and light, love becomes twisted and withered. Love needs acknowledgment to grow to full force. Let the light of God's love shine on you and your mate today and every day as you continue to stand together in love.

ECCLESIASTES 11:7

*Truly the light is sweet,*
*And it is pleasant for the eyes to behold the sun.*

# Harmony

Love is much like an orchestra responding
to the skill and care of a conductor.
No single instrument can ever be the sole
star. The harmony of all players working
together is what makes the piece a thing of
beauty. Live in that kind of harmony with
your spouse. If there is discord in your
heart, conduct it out today.

## 1 CORINTHIANS 13:4-5

*Love suffers long and is kind; love does not envy;*
*love does not parade itself, is not puffed up;*
*does not behave rudely, does not seek its own,*
*is not provoked, thinks no evil.*

# Living with Hope

## Shower

Lift your eyes to the Lord of the heavens and ask Him to shower your love relationship with grace. He is the One who enables you to love. It is He who gives you more ability to love if you ask Him. May His love encompass you and your beloved today.

### PSALM 72:6

*He shall come down like rain
upon the grass before mowing,
Like showers that water the earth.*

# Kisses

Drink your fill of the kisses of your
beloved. Savor the warmth of your
lover's closeness. God smiles to see the
love you share with your mate.
Rejoice in your life together.

## SONG OF SOLOMON 1:2

*Let him kiss me with the kisses of his mouth—*
*For your love is better than wine.*

# Shield

When enemies are camped around
you and your beloved, do not fear.
The God who reigns over all the earth
and heavens will be your Defender
and will shield you from harm.

## PSALM 91:4

*He shall cover you with His feathers,*
*And under His wings you shall take refuge;*
*His truth shall be your shield and buckler.*

# Capacity

Loving someone is not always easy.
Everyone has blocks that often stand in
the way. Too many old hurts make us
cautious in love. Ask God to continue to
bring you to maturity and give you the
capacity to love as never before.

### PHILIPPIANS 1:6

*Being confident of this very thing,*
*that He who has begun a good work in you*
*will complete it until the day of Jesus Christ.*

# Center

Center your heart around God and He
will give you the desires of your heart.
Come to God with your mate and
dedicate your love to Him. Thank Him
for giving you your life's companion.

## PROVERBS 3:5-6

*Trust in the LORD with all your heart,*
*And lean not on your own understanding;*
*In all your ways acknowledge Him,*
*And He shall direct your paths.*

# Acceptance

Love your mate with confidence.
Support your beloved's strengths but
don't shy away from the weaknesses.
They are all part of being human.
Believe the best of your mate even
as you accept their frailness.

1 CORINTHIANS 13:4, 7

*Love suffers long and is kind . . . bears all things,*
*believes all things, hopes all things,*
*endures all things.*

# Precious

Give the precious gift of your heart to
God first and then to your beloved.
Do not hold back. Give of yourself freely
without counting the price. You'll be
rewarded over and over for your efforts.

## PROVERBS 3:15

*She is more precious than rubies,*
*And all the things you may desire*
*cannot compare with her.*

# Learning

Marriage is a great teacher. You see your own
faults more clearly when placed up against
another's needs. Thank God for His help as you
grow into the person He wants you to be. Life is
your school, and your mate is one of your best
teachers. Learn well today and every day.

### JUDE 24

*Now to Him who is able to keep you from stumbling,*
*And to present you faultless*
*Before the presence of His glory with exceeding joy.*

# Blessings

When people receive a great gift, they usually cannot wait to tell everyone they know about it. Your mate is one of God's greatest blessings to you. Make sure other people know of your regard for your beloved. Don't keep your beloved's good qualities a secret. Speak of your blessings to others.

## MATTHEW 5:8

*Blessed are the pure in heart,*
*For they shall see God.*

# Sweetness

Let your mind savor sweetness, whether it is a sweet thought of your beloved or a sweet moment with the Lord. Soak your being in love, and let affection be the hallmark that describes your life.

## PROVERBS 16:21

*The wise in heart will be called prudent,*
*And sweetness of the lips increases learning.*

# Facing
# Hard Times

## *Fortress*

Love is a fortress against trouble
from all sides. It will withstand fierce
storms if your relationship is sturdy
and strong. Be strong together.

### PROVERBS 15:17

*Better is a dinner of herbs where love is,*
*Than a fatted calf with hatred.*

# Oneness

Develop a sense of oneness with your partner. Use disagreements to build your relationship by talking about problems when they occur. Don't let resentment become a wedge between you. If you do, it can split you apart.

## MARK 3:25

*And if a house is divided against itself,
that house cannot stand.*

# Consideration

Make sure your actions match your words.
Don't tell someone, "I love you, oh, how I
love you," and then neglect to demonstrate
this love in action and deed. Be kind and
considerate with your loved one.

## 1 Corinthians 13:1

*Though I speak with the tongues of men
and of angels, but have not love,
I have become sounding brass
or a clanging cymbal.*

# Commit

Commit yourself to the promises of God
in the hard times. Don't give way to a
bottomless pit of despair. Talk to God about
your feelings. Remind Him of the promises
He has made to His people—to you.

## JAMES 1:12

*Blessed is the man who endures temptation;*
*for when he has been approved,*
*he will receive the crown of life*
*which the Lord has promised to those who love Him.*

# Love

Don't underestimate the power of love
to see you through hard times.
Faith and hope are vital. But the Bible
tells us that love continues to win the
day. Tell your mate of your love even
more when the hard times come.

## 1 CORINTHIANS 13:13

*And now abide faith, hope, love, these three;
but the greatest of these is love.*

# Quietness

Be grateful for those times with your
mate that are filled with richness,
quietness, and contentment. Don't let
the pursuit of money or fame become a
substitute for spending time nourishing
your love relationship.

### Isaiah 30:15

*In returning and rest you shall be saved;*
*In quietness and confidence shall be your strength.*

# Positive

Look for times in your love relationship when you can speak a word of encouragement or praise. Don't hesitate to tell of the joy you share with your loved one. Positive words strengthen your bond of love.

## PROVERBS 15:23

*A man has joy by the answer of his mouth,*
*And a word spoken in due season, how good it is!*

# Secrets

Be careful about having secrets from
your mate. Learn to be open and
vulnerable. Openness develops trust and
trust builds love. Ask God for courage
to be transparent with the one you love.

PROVERBS 9:17-18

*"Stolen water is sweet,*
*And bread eaten in secret is pleasant."*
*But he does not know that the dead are there,*
*That her guests are in the depths of hell.*

# Frustration

Being angry is not a sin. However, be
careful that your anger does not lead you
to sin. Talk about your fears,
frustrations, and hurts with your beloved.
Don't hold your anger inside.

## EPHESIANS 4:26

*"Be angry, and do not sin":*
*do not let the sun go down on your wrath.*

# Tenderness

True love outlasts the most difficult of
times. Nourish your love in the hard times.
It will make your troubles more bearable.
Learn to stand close to your beloved when
storms shake your household.

## EPHESIANS 4:31-32

*Let all bitterness, wrath, anger, clamor,*
*and evil speaking be put away from you,*
*with all malice.*
*And be kind to one another, tenderhearted,*
*forgiving one another,*
*even as God in Christ forgave you.*

# Growing

## with God

### Changes

If you are impatient with God's working in
your love relationship, tell Him the concerns
of your heart right now. Tell Him you want
a meaningful, mutually fulfilling relationship
with your spouse. Ask for wisdom to make
your love stronger each day.

PSALM 119:124-125

*Deal with Your servant according to Your mercy,*
*And teach me Your statutes.*
*I am Your servant;*
*Give me understanding,*
*That I may know Your testimonies.*

# Vulnerable

Honesty is one of the most vital
ingredients to a love relationship. If you
are afraid of being fully known by your
beloved, practice by first being vulnerable
before God. Share deeply with Him.
Tell Him things unknown to others.
Once you feel His boundless acceptance,
you'll be better prepared to be honest
with your beloved.

PSALM 139:23-24

*Search me, O God, and know my heart;*
*Try me, and know my anxieties;*
*And see if there is any wicked way in me,*
*And lead me in the way everlasting.*

# Cuddle

Does your beloved seem far away, lost in concerns and problems? Everyone feels alone at times—uncared for and seemingly without a friend. Remember, that's one of the best times to draw close to God. Literally see yourself cradled in His arms. He is your friend and constant companion. Then, take that spirit of God's love and share it with your mate. Enjoy an evening of cuddling . . . of just being together.

JAMES 4:8

*Draw near to God and He will draw near to you.*

# Devotions

Set aside a time to read God's Word with
your beloved. As your souls grow closer to
the Spirit of God, you will find yourselves
growing closer to each other. Make daily
shared devotions a vital part of your
relationship and your spiritual growth.

## HEBREWS 4:16

*Let us therefore come boldly
to the throne of grace,
that we may obtain mercy
and find grace to help in time of need.*

# Loyalty

The loyalty you feel for your beloved
is precious beyond words. Tell your
mate you will stand fast all the way.
It's easy to be gracious when you're
riding the crest of personal success.
Be there for the hard times too.

## RUTH 1:16

*For wherever you go, I will go;*
*And wherever you lodge, I will lodge;*
*Your people shall be my people,*
*And your God, my God.*

# Openness

Speak your emotions freely but gently.
Your love will flourish as a result of the
honest outpouring of your heart. The same is
true in your relationship with God.
He wants you to tell Him how you feel.
Speak your mind. Share your heart. God will
listen and comfort you in all your ways.

## PSALM 119:145

*I cry out with my whole heart;*
*Hear me, O LORD!*
*I will keep Your statutes.*

# Choice

You can't earn love. Love is a gift. You can't
buy love. It's simply not for sale. And it is
especially true for God's love. God has given
us love because He has chosen to do so.
No one has ever been good enough to
receive love. We love simply because we
choose to love. Unconditional love is the
most powerful force on earth.

## 1 John 4:7

*Beloved, let us love one another, for love is of God;
and everyone who loves is born of God
and knows God.*

# Equals

The Bible says we are all equally precious in the eyes of God. Put your beloved's concerns on an equal footing with your own. Search for the best in your spouse. In so doing, your love relationship will flourish. Enjoy the dream of staying in love—forever.

## GALATIANS 3:28

*There is neither Jew nor Greek,*
*there is neither slave nor free,*
*there is neither male nor female;*
*for you are all one in Christ Jesus.*

# Reflections

Share your deepest reflections with your
beloved. Talk often of the things on your
mind and your heart. The more you
share, the closer you'll come to each
other in love and understanding.
Give the one you love the gift of yourself.

## PSALM 139:17

*How precious also are Your thoughts to me, O God!*
*How great is the sum of them!*

# Togetherness

The Bible says the harmony of your
love life affects the working of your
prayers. God does not respond to your
supplications the same if you pray from
one side of your mouth while fighting
with your mate out the other. Let your
life together be one of harmony.

## 1 PETER 3:7

*Husbands, likewise, dwell with them*
*with understanding,*
*giving honor to the wife, as to the weaker vessel,*
*and as being heirs together of the grace of life,*
*that your prayers may not be hindered.*

# Rejoicing
## *in* Abundance

## *Growing*

The Lord of all the heavens and earth has

blessed you with His love and care.

He delights in pleasing you throughout your

days and in helping you and your beloved

grow to full stature and strength.

### Psalm 13:6

*I will sing to the Lord,*

*Because He has dealt bountifully with me.*

# Overflowing

Give and it shall be given back to you,
pressed down and overflowing. An open
heart and a gentle open hand are the
best insurance of a long and lasting
love affair with your mate.

## PROVERBS 11:25

*The generous soul will be made rich,*
*And he who waters will also be watered himself.*

# Anointing

God rains down His anointing power on His people. If you or your spouse have any lack, go to the Father who knows your every need. He will open His great storehouse of blessings and shower you with His generous heart.

## PSALM 23:5-6

*You anoint my head with oil;*
*My cup runs over.*
*Surely goodness and mercy shall follow me*
*All the days of my life;*
*And I will dwell in the house of the LORD*
*Forever.*

# Gifts

If you and your spouse were to count all the wondrous things God has done for you, you would be overwhelmed. He gives you life, sustenance, and His all-abiding love. He also has given you a mind and a heart to appreciate all He has given.

## PSALM 68:19

*Blessed be the Lord,*
*Who daily loads us with benefits,*
*The God of our salvation!*

# Hang On

Get a grip on hope and hang on tight.
Hope is the rope that rescues us from
despair and lethargy. Hang on tight
and keep expecting God to work a
miracle in your life.

## PSALM 71:14

*But I will hope continually,*
*And will praise You yet more and more.*

# Praise

Compliments bring a sparkle to everyone's eyes. Look for reasons to compliment your beloved. Notice the fabric of your spouse's personality and give all the encouragement and praise you can.

## PROVERBS 15:30

*The light of the eyes rejoices the heart,*
*And a good report makes the bones healthy.*

# Unmeasured

Love your mate with abandonment.
Don't measure your love and weigh what
you receive in return. Be a lover who gives
yourself today with no thought for the hurts
of the past or the problems of the future.

## LUKE 6:38

*Give, and it will be given to you:*
*good measure, pressed down, shaken together,*
*and running over will be put into your bosom.*

# Favor

God has put His loving hand on the
pulse of your life, and He has given you
wondrous gifts. Thank Him for the gift
of love He has given to you through
your special mate.

## PROVERBS 18:22

*He who finds a wife finds a good thing,*
*And obtains favor from the LORD.*

# Enjoy

Savor each day and drink of its sweetness.

Treasure each moment of vibrant life the

Lord has given to you. Don't wile your

hours or days away waiting for what will be.

Enjoy what is. Do it now!

## PSALM 118:24

*This is the day the LORD has made;*
*We will rejoice and be glad in it.*

# Prosper

Lift your arms to the sky and thank God
for the sunshine He has given to you.
Every ounce of energy you have has been
given to you by Him. Rejoice in the
abundance of health and wealth He has
given you and your beloved.

## 3 JOHN 1:2

*Beloved, I pray that you may prosper
in all things and be in health,
just as your soul prospers.*

# Building a Family

## Children

If you yearn for children and have none of your own, come to God in prayer. God delights in giving you good things. Ask Him to bless you with a child to love and cherish.

### PSALM 127:3

*Behold, children are a heritage from the LORD,*
*The fruit of the womb is a reward.*

# Example

If you want your child to grow to be a God-fearing adult, then you and your mate need to show your child what God-fearing people live like. There is no substitute for a loving example. Be an example of God's love today.

## 1 TIMOTHY 4:12

*Let no one despise your youth,*
*but be an example to the believers*
*in word, in conduct, in love, in spirit,*
*in faith, in purity.*

# *Law*

It is important to teach your child the law and
the love of God. Read the scriptures together
as a family. Give your child a chance to ask
questions about your own beliefs. Say in
words he can understand what God has done
in the life of you and your mate.

## PROVERBS 1:8-9

*My son, hear the instruction of your father,*
*And do not forsake the law of your mother;*
*For they will be a graceful ornament on your head,*
*And chains about your neck.*

# Discipline

Discipline is a difficult area for many
families. Discuss with your mate how you
both wish to deal with the various
challenges of raising children. Then be firm
and compassionate in your daily discipline,
always speaking the truth in love.

## PROVERBS 3:12

*For whom the LORD loves He corrects,*
*Just as a father the son in whom he delights.*

# Training

Have hope as you nurture your child.
The Bible says the early training will
abide with your sons and daughters even
when they become old. Make it a habit
to talk with your child, at an early age,
about God's love.

## PROVERBS 22:6

*Train up a child in the way he should go,*
*And when he is old he will not depart from it.*

# Faith

Faith is contagious. When your spouse and you speak of your faith and live it in your everyday lives, your child will be influenced by its power. Show your child how to have faith today.

## ROMANS 10:17

*So then faith comes by hearing, and hearing by the word of God.*

# Truth

Teach your children to tell the truth.
A respect for honesty will serve them
well throughout their entire lives. Be
sure to speak the truth yourself in your
dealings with others. Your children will
see it and follow your example.

## 3 JOHN 1:4

*I have no greater joy
than to hear that my children walk in truth.*

# Gentleness

Guide your children with gentleness and kindness. Show your children kindness from an early age and train them with a godly affection. Even when you must discipline, be sure your children know they are loved simply for who they are.

## PHILIPPIANS 4:5

*Let your gentleness be known to all men.*
*The Lord is at hand.*

# *Obedience*

Teach your children to obey you.
Early lessons in respect for authority
provide your children with a firm
base for success in relationships with
others. When you are affectionate
with your children, it is easier for
them to want to do what you say.

### EPHESIANS 6:1

*Children, obey your parents in the Lord,
for this is right.*

# Legacy

Leave a legacy for your children. When you have children, you immediately begin to care more deeply about the welfare and feeding of the nation and our physical world. Talk with your spouse about what you two can do to help make our planet a better place for your children and grandchildren to live.

## PSALM 145:4

*One generation shall praise*
*Your works to another,*
*And shall declare Your mighty acts.*

## Philippians 1:9-11

*And this I pray,*

*that your love may abound still more and more*

*in knowledge and all discernment,*

*that you may approve the things that are excellent,*

*that you may be sincere and without offense
till the day of Christ,*

*being filled with the fruits of righteousness
which are by Jesus Christ,*

*to the glory and praise of God.*